ANIMAL RHYTHMS
ALPHABET

By Cindy McCord and Shirley Ross

Publisher: Roberta Suid
Editor: Mary McClellan
Design and production: Susan Cronin-Paris
Art: Susan Cronin-Paris and Shirley Ross
Cover Design: David Hale

ISBN 0-912107-69-3

Printed in the United States of America
8 7 6 5

INTRODUCTION

Animal alphabets have been around for a long time, but Animal Rhythms is special. It is designed to teach young children the letters of the alphabet and their sounds, using colorful animal puppets, appealing alliterative chants, feely letters, art projects, cooking and tasting experiences, related science and math activities, and lots of language arts ideas.

Animal Rhythms is specially designed to encourage and maintain that wonderful enthusiasm for learning that children exhibit when they first come to school. What children can resist puppets that they have made? How can they not respond to the curiosity that is stirred when they discover bear tracks on the floor one morning leading to a basket full of things that begin with "b"? Or how can they keep still when hearing cheers for Bobby Bear or Penguin Pete?

Animal Rhythms is a total readiness program. Using the alphabet as a base, it coordinates many areas of the curriculum, enriching the learning experience and making it more meaningful. Its materials can be used alone or in conjunction with almost any other program. Though arranged alphabetically, the letters may be presented in any order suitable for the group of children who will be using the program.

A wide range of ideas is offered so that the program can be tailored to meet the needs of a variety of young learners. You can pick the activities that best suit your group of children.

Animal Rhythms is full of exciting materials. We hope that everyone who uses Animal Rhythms will enjoy the experience as much as the authors have enjoyed its creation.

Puppets

Children love puppets. Puppets become friends and playmates, and through them a variety of concepts can be explored.

What better way to encourage children to learn the sound of the letter "t" than to have them construct a puppet of Tiger Tim to take home, with the animal rhythm on the back and a bow tie under his chin with the letter "T t" written on it?

Patterns for Tiger Tim and all the other letter animals are included in this book. Construction pages for the puppets show a diagram of each puppet's face and list the patterns to use, with suggested colors and notes on construction details.

Duplicate the pattern pieces on lightweight cardboard stock, and cut them out. Use them as tracing patterns, or duplicate them on construction paper for the children to make into their puppets.

When the puppet's face is assembled and pasted together, staple it to a wooden tongue depressor. Or make a tube out of a piece of construction paper, and staple the animal to that.

In order to allow for each child's individual expression, children can cut freehand some of the parts of the animal faces, such as the eyes, nose, stripes, spots, and whiskers. As a result, each child's puppet will have unique characteristics. The patterns are included, however, for the teacher's use or for very young children who have not had much experience with cutting and pasting.

The puppets are fun to make, and they also provide practice of visual and small motor skills. In addition, each animal becomes a personal friend and treasured reminder of each letter and sound.

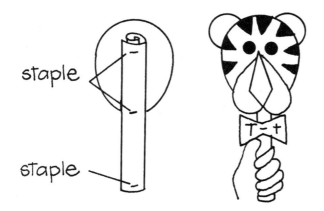

Rhythms

Teddy bear, Teddy bear, turn around.
Teddy bear, Teddy bear, touch the ground.
Teddy bear, Teddy bear, show your shoe.
Teddy bear, Teddy bear, that will do.

Playground and jump-rope chants are hard to forget. Every generation uses them, and somehow they never change. Their rhythms and special wording make them fun to say and easy to remember. It is with this in mind that the rhythmic, alliterative animal rhythms were created. They are designed to help children internalize the sounds of the alphabet letters as they occur at the beginning of words.

To teach a rhythm, say it over and over for the children, inviting them to join you when they are ready. Where the letter is repeated in the first and last line, say the letter name and then the sound.

Accompany each unit of study with many repetitions of the corresponding animal rhythm. Say the jingles with the beat and enthusiasm of a cheer at a football game. Chant them. Whisper them. March, clap, hop, jump, and shout them. Repeat them over and over. The repetitions will be fun, and the children will soon have them memorized.

Alphabet Activities

These activities are designed specifically for each letter and its sound. Use these pages to bring the Animal Rhythms program alive for your students. Included are ideas to introduce each letter study, experiences to develop the sound/letter concepts, and activities to integrate the program with the rest of the curriculum. These activities are meant to be used as a resource guide and a springboard for your own ideas. Use as many of the ideas as you can. Change them and add you own. Gluing marshmallows on the letter "m" for Moe Monkey and celebrating Bobby Bear's Beary Big Birthday Bash are experiences children won't forget.

Activity Page Contents

• The Attention Getter is a way to introduce the letter and its sound.
• The Collectables are real objects to use for display that begin with the sound being studied. (Pictures are okay, too.)
• The Language Pattern is a sentence to be completed with a word that begins with the appropriate sound and then used on pages that the children illustrate with drawings or pictures from magazines. Several pages together become a class book, or if each child does three or four, they can be made into individual sound books that can be taken home.

Fenton Fox is funny.
He likes feathers.

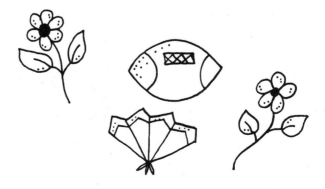

• The Celebration is a way to complete each letter/sound unit in style.

Tactile experiences help to reinforce letter/sound concepts. Have the children trace the letters in the air or form them with their bodies. Children love to choose a friend and take turns tracing letters on each other's back. Call these "tickle letters." There are ideas for making Feely Letters for each letter on the Alphabet Activity sheets. Beans, glitter, cereal, and marshmallows are all wonderful for children to work with.

Salt trays also provide good practice in letter formation and recognition. Fingerpainted letters are messy but fun. How about using shaving cream on a table? The children won't be able to take their writing home, but it will be a great experience.

Letter rubbings are another favorite activity. Sandpaper letters placed under paper and rubbed with the side of a crayon become very attractive pieces of letter art.

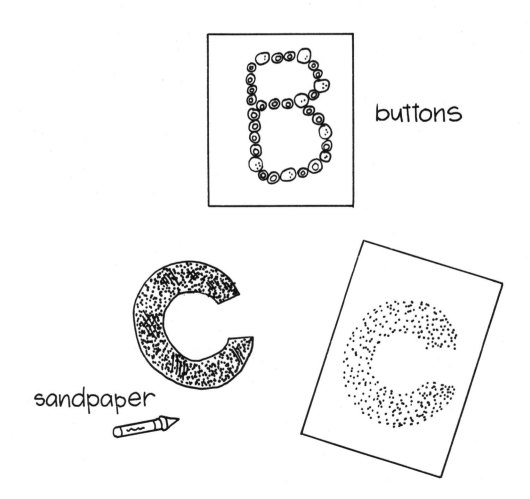

buttons

sandpaper

ALLIGATOR ANN

head	7	green	narrow end down
snout	22	green	
eyes	19	yellow	cut two
nostrils	20	black	cut one in half
spots		orange	cut freehand
teeth		white	cut freehand triangles

BOBBY BEAR

head	1	brown	narrow end up
ears	9	brown	show round end
muzzle	5	pink	
nose	20	black	
eyes	20	black	cut two
mouth	17	black	

CAMEL CAL

head	1	brown	narrow end down
ears	9	brown	pointed end down
muzzle	7	yellow	pointed end up
bangs	8	yellow	
eyes	19	white	cut two
pupils	20	black	cut two
eyelids	19	black	cut one in half
nose/ mouth		black	cut two thin strips freehand

DINOSAUR DAWN

head	1	green	narrow end up
mouth	16	yellow	
eyes	19	white	cut two
pupils	20	black	cut two
nostrils	20	yellow	cut two
plates	14	orange	cut four freehand triangles

ELEPHANT ED

head	1	pink	narrow end up
ears	3	turq	cut two
trunk	23	orange	
eyes	19	white	cut two
pupils	20	black	cut two

FENTON FOX

head	1	orange	narrow end down
ears	9	orange	show pointed end
face	7	white	pointed end down
eyes	20	green	
whiskers		black	cut freehand
nose	18	black	

GERTIE GOOSE

head	1	yellow	narrow end up
bill	4	orange	
bill top	17	dk blue	
eyes	19	white	cut two
pupils	20	black	cut two
nostrils	20	black	cut one in half

HIPPO HAL

head	1	turq	narrow end up
muzzle	3	blue	
ears	9	blue	rounded end up
eyes	19	white	cut two
pupils	20	black	cut two
nostrils	20	black	cut two

ICHABOD INDRI

head	1	black	narrow end down
ears	9	black	rounded end shows
muzzle	9	pink	pointed end up
nose	14	black	pointed end up
eyes	18	white	cut two
pupils	20	black	cut two

JAGUAR JAN

head	1	brown	narrow end down
jowls	7	yellow	pointed end up
ears	9	brown	rounded end shows
whiskers		black	cut freehand
nose	11	black	narrow end up
eyes	19	yellow	horizontal
pupils		black	cut freehand triangles
spots		black	cut freehand shapes

KATY KANGAROO

head	1	green	narrow end down
muzzle	6	purple	
ears	10	green	show pointed end
eyes	19	white	cut two
pupils	20	black	cut two
nose	20	black	
mouth	17	black	

LION LOU

head	1	brown	narrow end down
jowls	7	yellow	pointed end up
whiskers		black	cut freehand
nose	11	black	narrow end up
ears	9	brown	show round end
eyes	20	black	cut two
mane		orange	cut strips

MOE MONKEY

head	1	brown	narrow end down
face	7	white	pointed end down
muzzle	5	yellow	
ears	6	brown	vertical, cut two
eyes	20	black	cut two
nose line		black	narrow strip
nose	18	black	
mouth	17	black	

NARWHAL NED

head	1	dk blue	narrow end up
mouth	16	black	
eyes	19	white	cut two
pupils	20	black	cut two
horn	12	yellow	

OLIVER OSTRICH

head	2	purple	
cheeks	6	yellow	horizontal
beak	13	orange	horizontal
eyes	19	white	cut two
pupils	20	black	cut two
eyelids	19	black	cut one in half
nostrils	20	black	cut one in half

PENGUIN PETE

head	2	black	
beak	11	yellow	narrow end down
eyes	19	white	cut two
pupils	20	black	cut two

QUINCY QUAIL

head	2	turq	
face	7	orange	pointed end down
plume	10	orange	cut fringe
beak	15	yellow	narrow end down
eyes	19	white	cut two
pupils	20	black	cut two

RHINO RUTH

head	1	dk blue	narrow end up
muzzle	5	yellow	
horn	11	orange	narrow end up
ears	9	dk blue	show round end
eyes	19	white	cut two
pupils	20	black	cut two
nostrils	20	black	cut two

SUZY SEAL

head	2	black	
jowls	6	white	overlap in middle
nose	18	turq	
eyes	19	white	cut two
pupils	20	black	cut two
whiskers		black	cut freehand

TIGER TIM

head	1	orange	narrow end down
jowls	7	white	pointed end up
ears	9	orange	show round end
whiskers		black	cut freehand
nose	11	black	
eyes	20	black	cut two
stripes		black	cut freehand triangles

UMBRELLA BIRD

head	2	green	
wattle	9	purple	cut two
crest	8	purple	
beak	15	yellow	
eyes	20	black	cut two

VULTURE VIC

head	1	black	narrow end down
beak	7	orange	pointed end down
bangs	8	orange	
eyes	19	white	cut two
pupils	20	black	cut two
nostrils	20	black	cut one in half

WALRUS WALT

head	1	black	narrow end down
jowls	7	white	pointed end up, with fringe on curves
nose	18	turq	
eyes	19	white	cut two
pupils	20	black	cut two
tusks	12	purple	pointed end down

YOLANDA YAK

head	1	turq	narrow end up
face	11	white	pointed end up
muzzle	4	purple	
bangs	8	purple	
ears	10	turq	cut two
horns	21	white	cut two
beard	12	purple	point up, fringe bottom
eyes	19	black	cut two
nostrils	20	black	cut two

ZEBRA ZACH

head	1	white	narrow end up
muzzle	4	pink	
ears	10	black	one ear cocked
nose	12	black	pointed end up
mane	12	pink	pointed end down, fringe top
eyes	20	black	cut two
nostrils	20	black	cut two
stripes		black	cut freehand triangles

AMY APE

head	1	black	narrow end up
muzzle	5	purple	
face	7	white	point down
ears	9	black	show round side
eyes	20	black	
nose	20	black	
mouth	17	black	

EGRET EVE

head	1	dk blue	narrow end down
beak	11	yellow	narrow end down
eyes	20	black	

IBEX IKE

head	1	black	narrow end down
ears	10	black	cut two
muzzle	11	white	narrow end up
bangs	8	white	
beard	12	yellow	pointed side up, fringe bottom
horns	21	yellow	cut two
eyes	19	white	cut two
pupils	20	black	cut two
nose	19	black	

OLIVIA OPOSSUM

head	1	black	narrow end down
ears	9	pink	show pointed end
nose	18	pink	
eyes	18	pink	cut two
pupils	20	black	cut two

UNI UNICORN

head	1	turq	narrow end down
ears	10	turq	cut two
bangs	8	white	
mane	12	white	pointed end down
muzzle	6	white	
horn	12	pink	cut two
eyes	19	white	cut two
pupils	20	black	cut two
nostrils	20	black	cut two

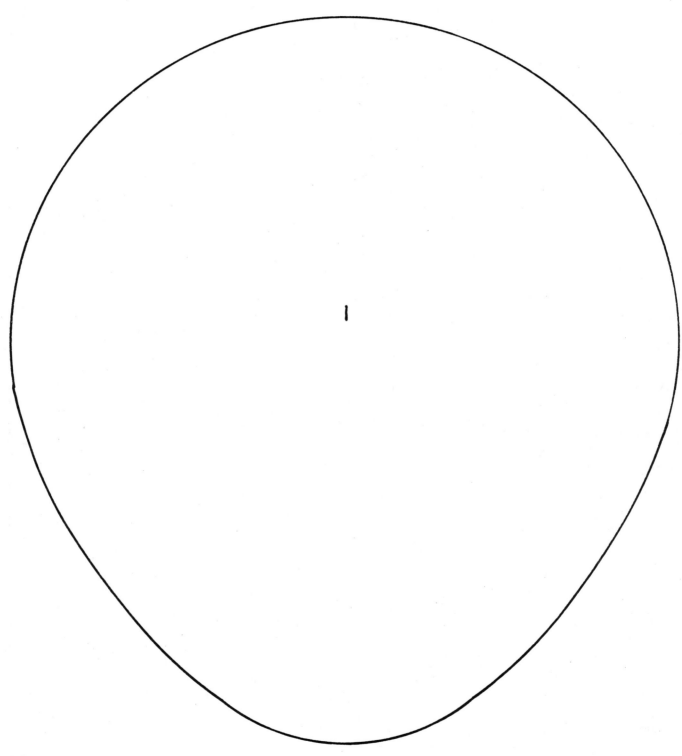

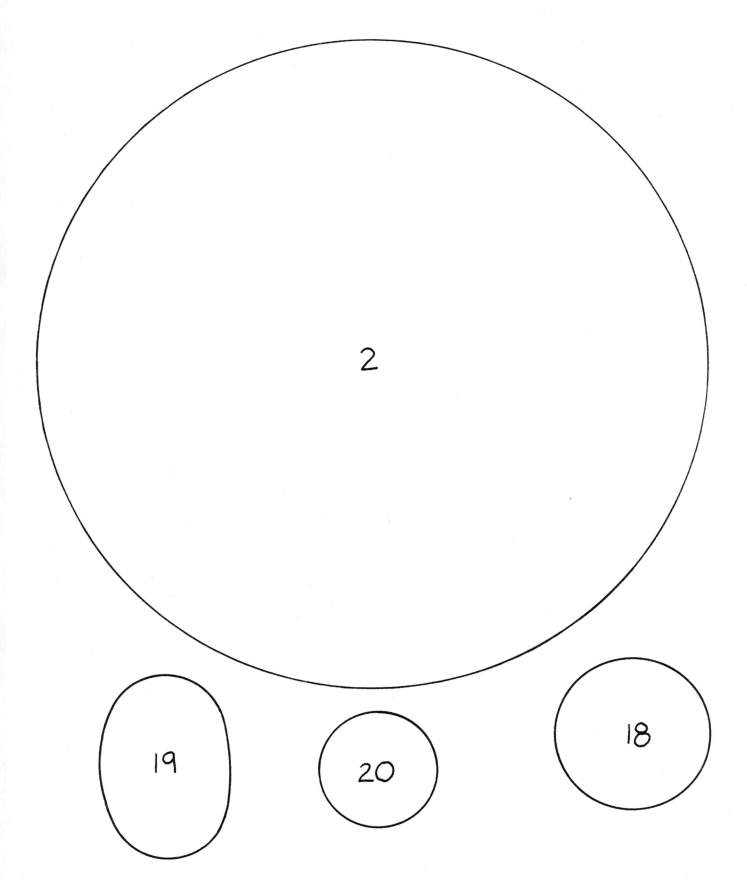

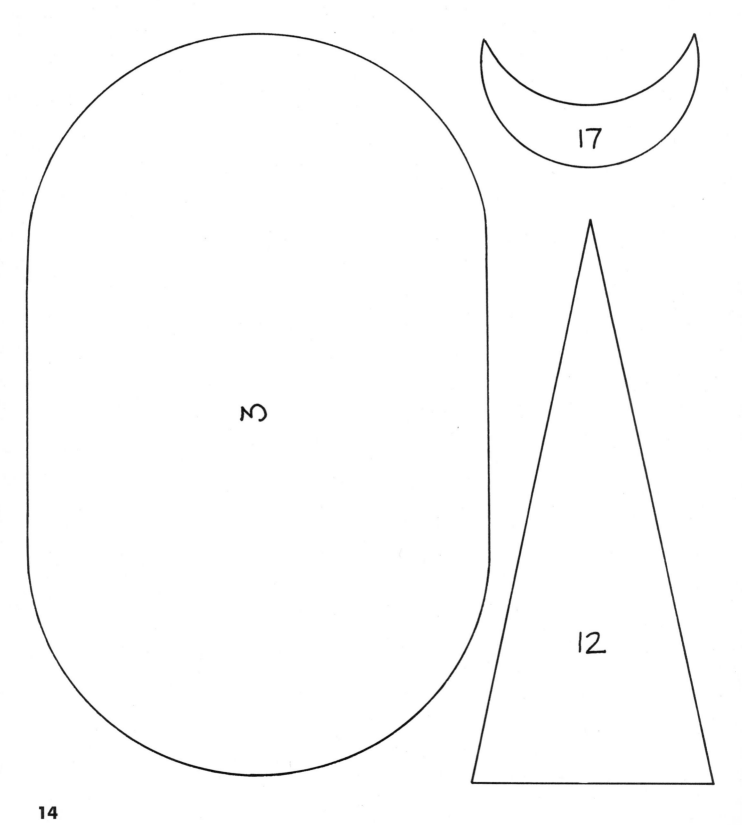

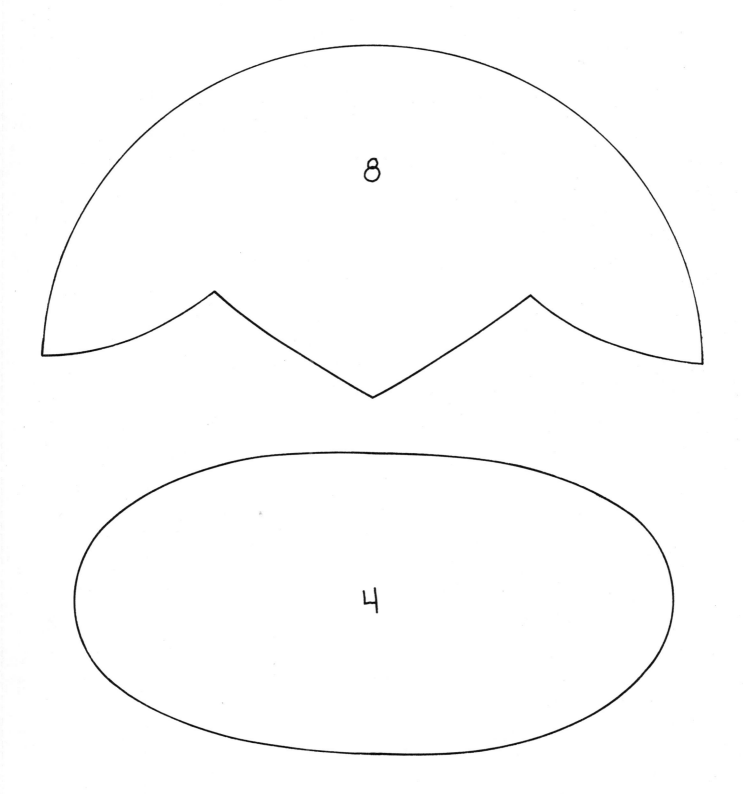

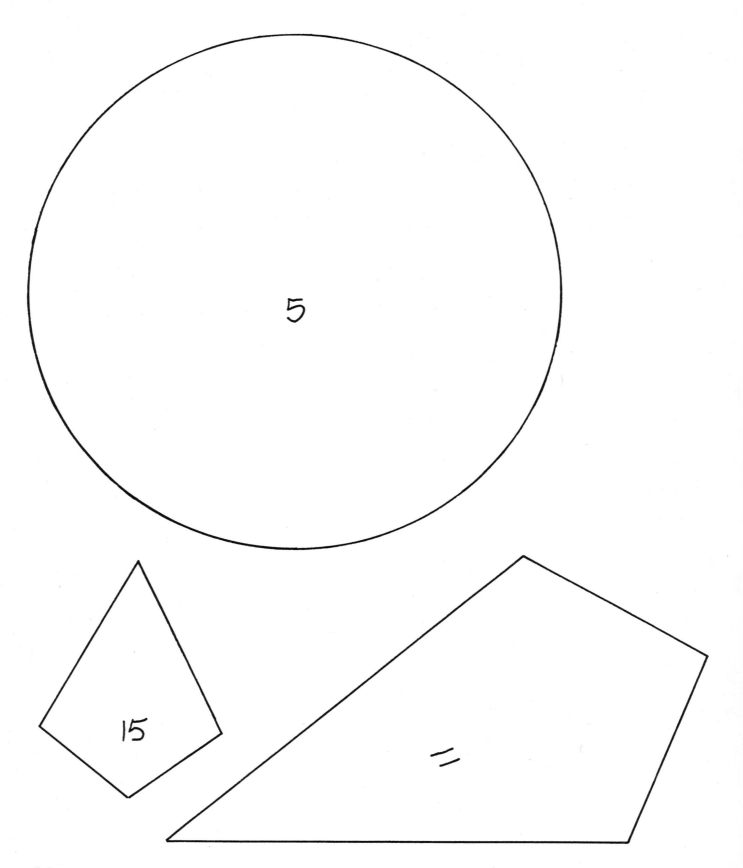

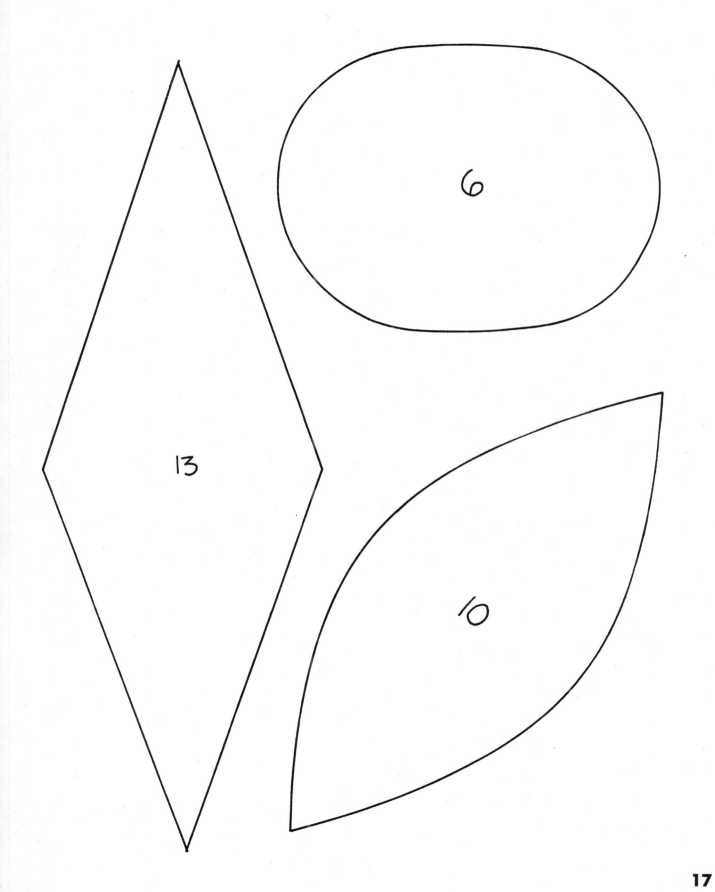

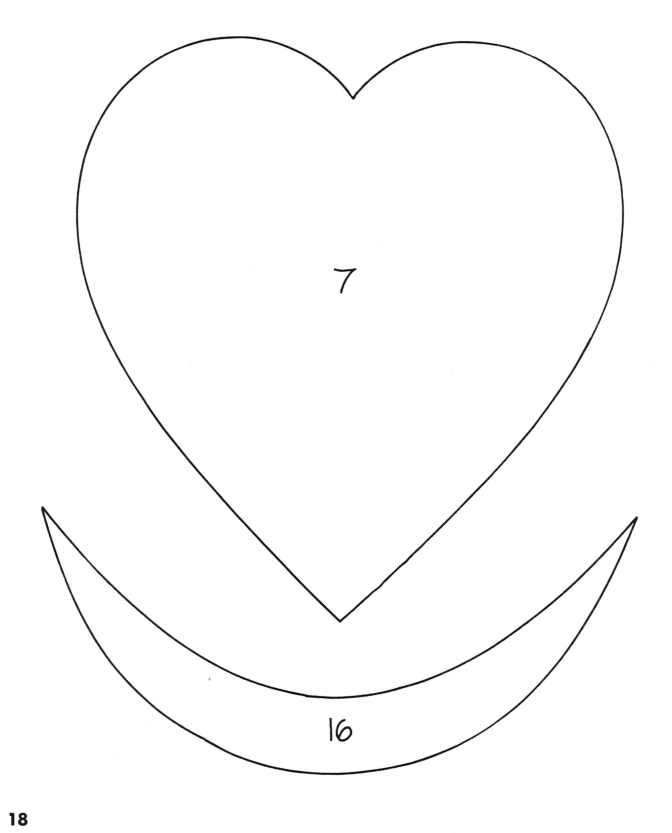

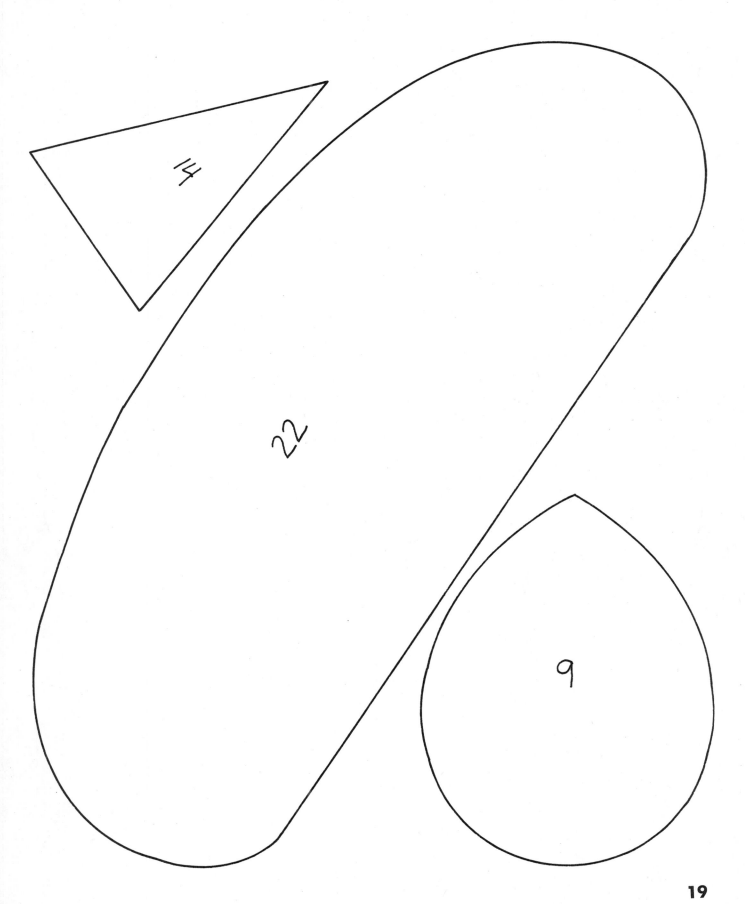

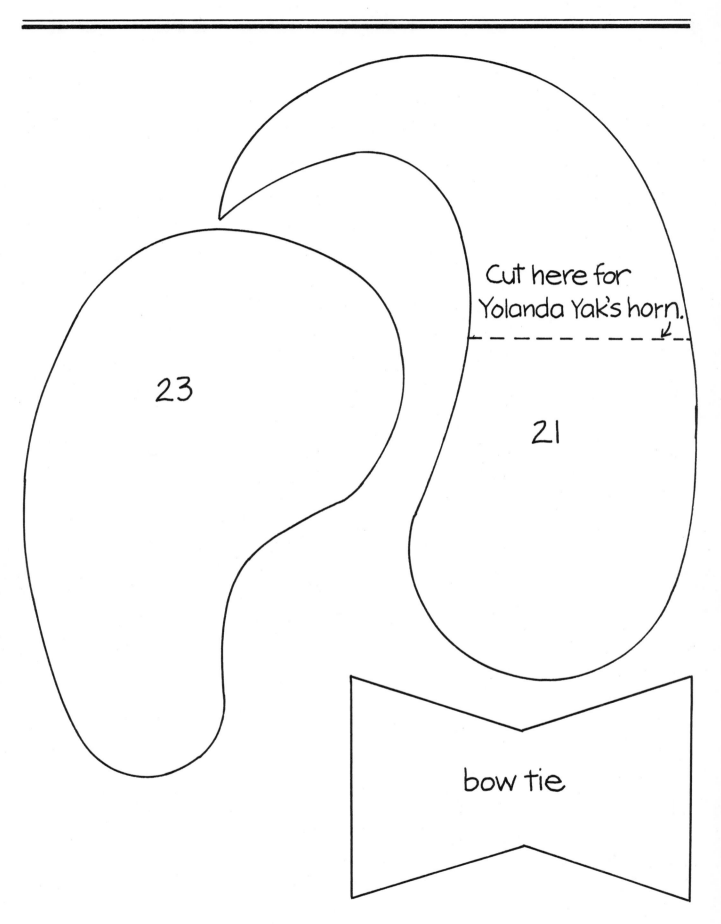

Cut here for
Yolanda Yak's horn.

23

21

bow tie

A a

A a for Amy Ape
Able angels aliens
Aprons acorns ancient age
A a for Amy Ape

I i

I i for Ibex Ike
Icy iron icicles
Irish ivy iodine
I i for Ibex Ike

My
Animal Rhythms
Alphabet

E e

E e for Egret Eve
Eating eels eagerly
Easy Easter evenings
E e for Egret Eve

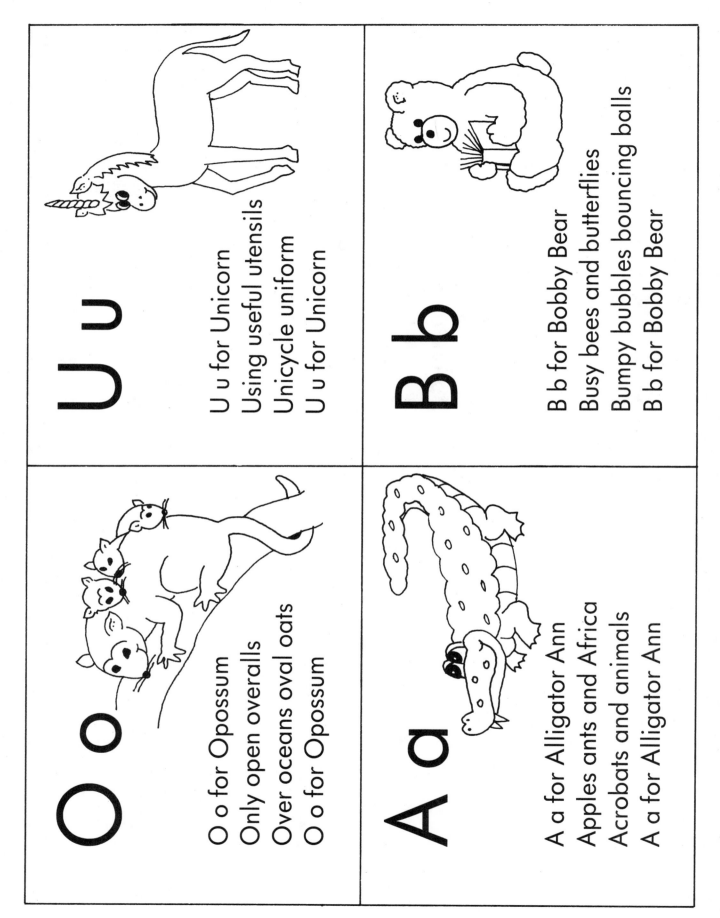

U u

U u for Unicorn
Using useful utensils
Unicycle uniform
U u for Unicorn

B b

B b for Bobby Bear
Busy bees and butterflies
Bumpy bubbles bouncing balls
B b for Bobby Bear

O o

O o for Opossum
Only open overalls
Over oceans oval oats
O o for Opossum

A a

A a for Alligator Ann
Apples ants and Africa
Acrobats and animals
A a for Alligator Ann

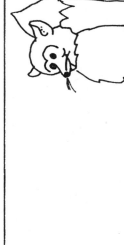

D d

D d for Dinosaur Dawn
Dancing dollies daffodils
Daddy dentist dingdong doors
D d for Dinosaur Dawn

F f

F f for Fenton Fox
Fiddle faddle five fat frogs
Fancy fishes food and fun
F f for Fenton Fox

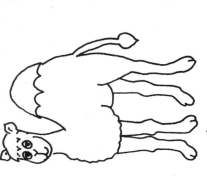

C c

C c for Camel Cal
Cookies cupcakes candy canes
Catching cactus carefully
C c for Camel Cal

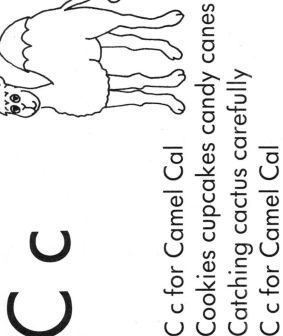

E e

E e for Elephant Ed
Every extra energy
Empty echoes exercise
E e for Elephant Ed

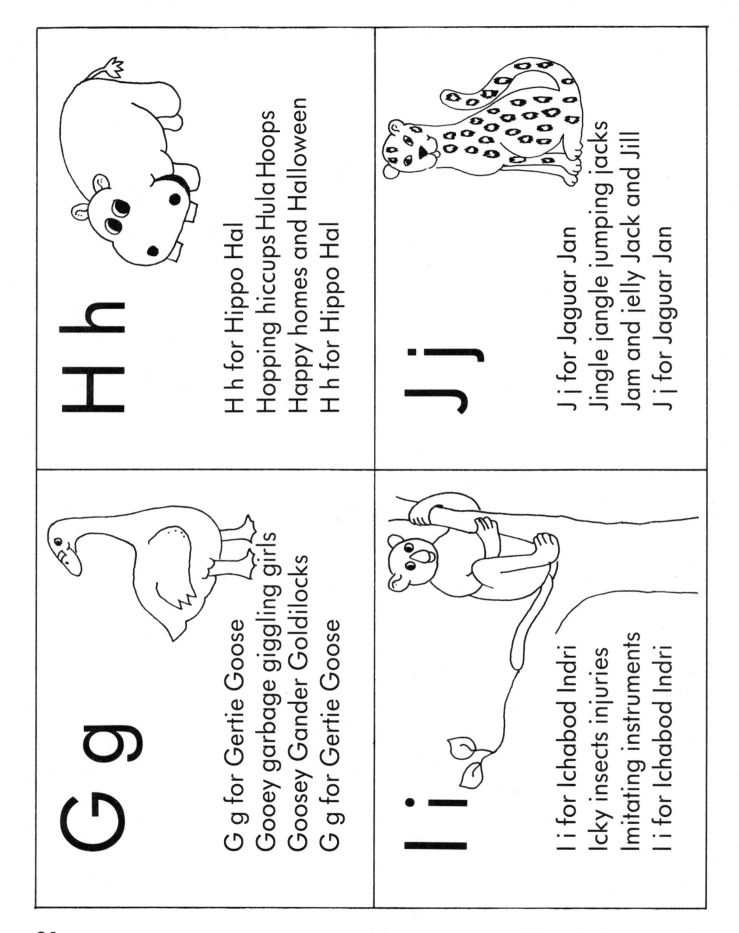

H h

H h for Hippo Hal
Hopping hiccups Hula Hoops
Happy homes and Halloween
H h for Hippo Hal

J j

J j for Jaguar Jan
Jingle jangle jumping jacks
Jam and jelly Jack and Jill
J j for Jaguar Jan

G g

G g for Gertie Goose
Gooey garbage giggling girls
Goosey Gander Goldilocks
G g for Gertie Goose

I i

I i for Ichabod Indri
Icky insects injuries
Imitating instruments
I i for Ichabod Indri

L l

L l for Lion Lou
Licking lemon lollipops
Letters love and ladybugs
L l for Lion Lou

N n

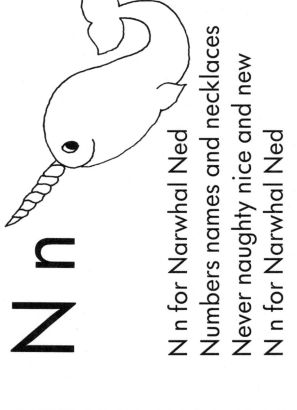

N n for Narwhal Ned
Numbers names and necklaces
Never naughty nice and new
N n for Narwhal Ned

K k

K k for Katy Kangaroo
Kindergarten kids and keys
Kittens kisses kindly kings
K k for Katy Kangaroo

M m

M m for Moe Monkey
Magic mittens marbles me
Macaroni mud and milk
M m for Moe Monkey

P p

P p for Penguin Pete
Puppies popcorn porcupines
Pitter-patter pumpkin pies
P p for Penguin Pete

R r

R r for Rhino Ruth
Rattles rocks and radios
Running races rockets roar
R r for Rhino Ruth

O o

O o for Oliver Ostrich
Octopus and operate
Oblong olives off and on
O o for Oliver Ostrich

Q q

Q q for Quincy Quail
Quiet queens and quarterbacks
Questions quilts and quarreling
Q q for Quincy Quail

T t

T t for Tiger Tim
Tummies toys and tambourines
Talking tables tattletales
T t for Tiger Tim

V v

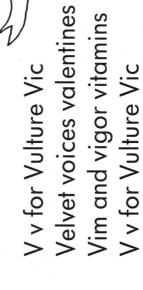

V v for Vulture Vic
Velvet voices valentines
Vim and vigor vitamins
V v for Vulture Vic

S s

S s for Suzy Seal
Scissors seesaw sandwiches
Silly soup and Saturday
S s for Suzy Seal

U u

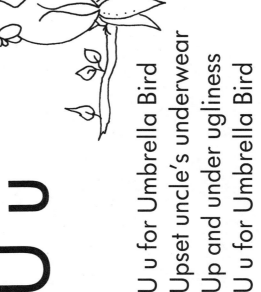
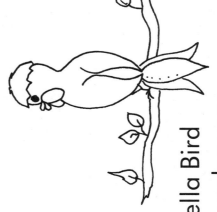

U u for Umbrella Bird
Upset uncle's underwear
Up and under ugliness
U u for Umbrella Bird

X x

There are not many words that begin with the letter x. Create an animal. Make up a name that begins with x.

Z z

Z z for Zebra Zach
Zooming zombies zinnias
Zigzag zippers zero zoo
Z z for Zebra Zach

W w

W w for Walrus Walt
Watermelons wonderful
Windy weather wiggling worms
W w for Walrus Walt

Y y

Y y for Yolanda Yak
Yippy yo-yos yummy yams
Yucky yellow yarn and you
Y y for Yolanda Yak

A a

COLLECTABLES

alfalfa seeds
alphabet
ambulance
animals
apples

astronaut
ax
āngel
āpron
āpricots

ATTENTION GETTER

- Sing the "Alphabet Song."
- Introduce Alligator Ann as an animal whose name begins with the short "a" sound.
- Give each child an alphabet to take home to practice.

FOOD FUN

- Cook applesauce.
- Bake angel food cake.
- Make ants on a log (raisins on celery sticks).

FEELY LETTERS

- Glue alphabet noodles on "a's."
- Glue alphabet cereal on "a's."

LANGUAGE

- Make Alligator Ann's Album full of "a" things.
- Pattern: Alligator Ann asks for an _____.

MUSIC

- Sing "The Ants Go Marching."
- Listen to an alto voice.

LITERATURE

- The Alphabet Tree, by Leo Lionni
- Johnny Appleseed, by Aliki
- Alexander, by Leo Lionni
- Anno's Alphabet, by Anno

ART

- Make apple prints.
- Make alphabet art. (Make letters into pictures, decorate letters, etc.)

MATH

- Graph apples according to color or size.

SOCIAL STUDIES

- Learn about astronauts.

SCIENCE

- Grow alfalfa sprouts.
- Learn about ants.
- Study alligators.
- Discuss apes.
- Study animals with antlers.

PHYSICAL EDUCATION

- Play at being airplanes.

CELEBRATION

- Alligator Ann's Apple Adventure: Choose some apple activities to do on this day.

B b

COLLECTABLES	
bag	beads
ball	beans
balloon	bell
banana	belt
bank	bottle
baseball	box
basket	brush

ATTENTION GETTER
- Put bear tracks on the floor leading to a basket full of things that begin with the "b" sound. Name each thing together. Discover the animal who brought them.
- Introduce Bobby Bear.

MUSIC
- Listen to bassoon music.
- Perform a ballet.
- Listen to a banjo or a bass singer.
- Sing "Bingo," "The Bear Went Over The Mountain," and "Teddy Bear, Teddy Bear."

LITERATURE
- <u>Berenstain Bears "B" Book</u>,
- <u>Brown Bear, Brown Bear</u>, by Bill Martin Jr.
- "The Three Bears," "Baa Baa Black Sheep," "Little Boy Blue," "Bye Baby Bunting"

LANGUAGE
- Brainstorm about big things.
- Pattern: B begins Bobby/ B begins Bear/ B begins _____, everywhere.

FOOD FUN
- Make bread, butter, biscuits, burritos, baked beans, or banana bread.
- Taste beets, broccoli, bagels, or berries.

SCIENCE
- Study birds, butterflies, or bees.
- Learn about bears.
- Find out about bubbles.

ART
- Make beautiful banners.
- Paint a picture by blowing paint around paper with a straw.
- Make blob-print butterflies.

FEELY LETTERS
- Make the letter "b" out of beans.

PHYSICAL EDUCATION
- Study birds, butterflies or bees.
- Have a balloon relay.
- Play some games with beanbags.
- Do balance activities.

MATH
- Classify buttons, beads, or beans.
- Make patterns with beads.
- Estimate the number of buttons or beans in a jar.

CELEBRATION
- Have a Beary Big Bash to culminate the study of the letter "b." Let the children bring their Teddy bears. Make a food that starts with "b." Blow some bubbles. Decorate with banners. Bring things that begin with "b"for sharing.

C c

ATTENTION GETTER

- Fill a cookie jar full of objects that begin with the sound of "c." Name each object as it is removed from the jar.
- Put a candy cane or cookie at each seat for the children to find when they arrive at school. Discuss who could have left them. Introduce Camel Cal.

SCIENCE

- Learn about camels or cactus.
- Make a crystal garden.
- Study color.
- Talk about caterpillars, cocoons, and chrysalises.

LANGUAGE

- Discuss what collections are.
- Pattern: Camel Cal counts 1, 2, 3. Camel Cal counts _____ with me.

LITERATURE

- Corduroy, by Don Freeman
- The Caboose Who Got Loose, by Bill Peet
- Caps for Sale, by Esphyr Slobodkina
- Crictor, by Tomi Ungerer

ART

- Work with clay.
- Create a collage.
- Make a crayon resist picture.

FEELY LETTERS

- Glue cotton balls in the shape of the letter "c."
- Write "c's" in shaving cream sprayed on tables.

CELEBRATION

- Culminate the unit with Camel Cal's Clown Carnival. Dress up like clowns. Create clown faces for an art project or with makeup. Cook something that begins with "c" for refreshments.

PHYSICAL EDUCATION

- Practice catching skills.

FOOD FUN

- Make carrot salad, cocoa, cookies, custard, carrot cake, cupcakes, carmel corn, cranberry sauce, or cole slaw.

SOCIAL STUDIES

- Discuss Christmas.

MUSIC

- Listen to a clarinet. Look at some pictures of one.

MATH

- Learn about the clock and calendar.

D d

COLLECTABLES

COLLECTABLES

daffodil	dog
daisy	doll
diamond	dollar
diaper	dollhouse
dime	donkey
dinosaur	dress
dirt	drum

ATTENTION GETTER
- Before school, hide things that begin with "d." Choose some detectives to look for them. Decide, based on the clues, what animal friend hid them.
- Introduce Dinosaur Dawn.

FOOD FUN
- Taste dates.
- Make doughnuts from refrigerator biscuit dough.

FEELY LETTERS
- Make "d's" out of dough.

LANGUAGE
- Pattern: Dinosaur Dawn devours _____.
- Make a dictionary of "d" things.

MUSIC
- Listen to some drum music.

LITERATURE
- Danny and the Dinosaur, by Sid Hoff
- "Diddle, Diddle Dumpling" and "Ding Dong Bell"

ART
- Make doodle designs.
- Do some drawings.
- Create dip and dye designs.

MATH
- Introduce dimes and dollars.
- Do some dot-to-dot drawings.
- Make a graph of dog owners.
- Learn about the diamond shape.

SOCIAL STUDIES
- Talk about doctors and dentists.
- Discuss daddies.

SCIENCE
- Study dinosaurs.
- Learn about deserts.
- Find out how to take care of a dog.

PHYSICAL EDUCATION
- Play Duck, Duck, Goose or Dodge Ball.

CELEBRATION
- Let children bring dolls to display for Dinosaur Dawn's Doll Day.

E e

COLLECTABLES

egg
elephant
elf
emblem
emery board
encyclopedia
engine

engineer
envelope
earring
eagle
Easter egg
eel

ATTENTION GETTER

- Display an egg carton full of plastic eggs. Put a picture of something that begins with "e" in all but one. One should remain empty. Open each one, name the picture, and point to the empty one. Guess the animal friend whose name begins with the same sound as the objects.
- Introduce Elephant Ed.

FOOD FUN

- Taste eggplant.
- Make egg salad. Save the eggshells for "Feely Letters."
- Make eclairs.

LANGUAGE

- Pattern: Elephant Ed enjoys
  _____.

LITERATURE

- Green Eggs and Ham, by Dr. Seuss
- Eat, by Diane Paterson

ART

- Make some crayon etchings.
- Design an emblem to wear.

FEELY LETTERS

- Glue crushed eggshells on letter "e's."

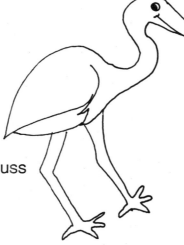

SCIENCE

- Study elephants and egrets.
- Learn about echoes, eggs, eels, and eagles.

MATH

- Do some estimating.

SOCIAL STUDIES

- Learn about Eskimos.
- Study engineers.

MUSIC

- Sing "Little Sir Echo."

PHYSICAL EDUCATION

- Do some exercises.

CELEBRATION

- Have Elephant Ed's "Eggstravaganza." Cook eggs (colored green) for refreshments.

F f

COLLECTABLES

fan	flowers
feather	flour
fig	football
file	fork
fish	frog
flag	frying pan
flashlight	funnel

ATTENTION GETTER
- Fill a fishbowl full of things that begin with the sound of "f." Name each one, and then introduce Fenton Fox.

FOOD FUN
- Let each child bring a piece of fruit to prepare and mix together for Friendship Fruit Salad.
- Make funny face sandwiches.
- Fudge is fun to prepare.

MATH
- Graph the fruit brought for the salad by favorite fruit or color.
- Sort fruit according to whether they contain one seed, many seeds, or no seeds.
- Practice counting four and five things.

LANGUAGE
- Make up a story about things that fly.
- Pattern: Fenton Fox is funny. He likes _____.

MUSIC
- Learn about folk songs.
- Listen to a French horn and a flute.
- Sing "Farmer in the Dell" and "Old MacDonald Had a Farm."

LITERATURE
- Fire! Fire! said Mrs. McQuire, by Bill Martin
- Frederick, by Leo Lionni
- Do You Want to be My Friend? by Eric Carle.

ART
- Fingerpaint modern art masterpieces.

CELEBRATION
- Culminate the study of Fenton Fox's letter by having Fenton Fox's Fabulous Fair. Hold a funny face or funny feet parade.

FEELY LETTERS
- Make "f's" with fingerprints.

PHYSICAL EDUCATION
- Make a paper plate Frisbee and fly it.

SOCIAL STUDIES
- Discuss fire fighters.
- Learn about friendship.
- Talk about families.
- Look at pictures of different flags.

SCIENCE
- Study feathers.
- Learn about fish, foxes, and frogs.
- Study flowers.
- Find out about fingerprints.

G g

COLLECTABLES

garlic	goggles
ghost	gold
gift	goldfish
glass	grapefruit
globe	grapes
glove	guitar
glue	gum

ATTENTION GETTER

- Put sugarless gum at each child's place. Think of different animals whose names begin with the same sound as "gum." Introduce Gertie Goose.
- Put "g" things in a gift box.

FEELY LETTERS

- Glue gold glitter on "g's"
- Make the "g's" with gumdrops glued on cardboard.

LANGUAGE

- Pattern: If I were Gertie Goose, I'd give _____ to girls.

MUSIC

- Listen to guitar music. Look at pictures of a guitar and learn about it.

LITERATURE

- Carrie Hepple's Garden, by Ruth Craft and Irene Haas

ART

- Make goofy goggles out of two connected cups from egg cartons.
- Do gadget printing designs.

MATH

- Count, sort, and graph gumdrops.

SOCIAL STUDIES

- Discuss grandparents.

CELEBRATION

- Have a game day. Children bring board games to play at school. Play group games outside.

SCIENCE

- Plant a garden.
- Learn about geese and goats.

PHYSICAL EDUCATION

- Do some galloping.

FOOD FUN

- Taste some goat cheese or goat's milk.
- Smell garlic.
- Make granola or gorp (raisins, peanuts, coconut, and chocolate bits).

H h

COLLECTABLES

hair	heart
hamburger	helicopter
hammer	hinge
hamster	hook
handkerchief	horn
hanger	horse
harmonica	hose
hat	house

ATTENTION GETTER
- A hat full of objects that begin with "h" introduces Hippo Hal. Ask how all the objects are alike and who would have hid them.

FEELY LETTERS
- Provide cut-out "h's" for the children to punch holes in (with a hole punch) or glue holes on "h's."

LANGUAGE
- Talk about different ways to say "Hello" (other English phrases, other languages, nonverbal).
- Language pattern: Hippo Hal is happy to have his
  _____.

MUSIC
- Listen to harp music.
- Play a harmonica.
- Do the Hokey Pokey.

LITERATURE
- Old Hat, New Hat, by Berenstains
- Arthur's Honey Bear, by Lillian Hoban

SCIENCE
- Discuss good health.
- Learn about hibernation.
- Talk about the heart.

PHYSICAL EDUCATION
- Practice hopping.
- Play hopscotch.
- Use Hula Hoops.
- Play Drop the Handkerchief.

CELEBRATION
- Hippo Hal's Hat Holiday: The children all wear hats to school.

FOOD FUN
- Make hot dogs.
- Taste honey and honeycomb.

MATH
- How many in a handful? Take a handful of small objects. Estimate how many in a handful.
- Study the concept of a half.

SOCIAL STUDIES
- Discuss hats people wear in different jobs.
- Learn about homes.
- Talk about hospitals.
- Discuss holidays: Halloween and Hanukkah.

ART
- Make handprints.
- Cut out hearts. Make designs or animals with them.
- Make hats.

I i

COLLECTABLES

igloo	īce
iguana	īcicle
incense	īris
initials	īsland
ink	īvy
insect	

ATTENTION GETTER

- Introduce the short "i" sound by describing the animal called the indri (in' dri). The indri belongs to the lemur primate family. It lives in Madagascar in tall trees and is rarely seen.

FEELY LETTERS

- Use ink to make letter "i's." Use ballpoint pens or marking pens.

FOOD FUN

- Make ice cream or icing to put on cupcakes.

LANGUAGE

- Brainstorm about things that are invisible. Make a chart or book of them.
- Patterns: Ichabod Indri is interested in _____.

MUSIC

- Learn about musical instruments.

LITERATURE

- Inch by Inch, by Leo Lionni
- Ira Sleeps Over, by Bernard Waber

SCIENCE

- Study ice.
- Learn about the indri.
- Study insects.
- Learn about the ibex.

CELEBRATION

- Plan Ichabod Indri's Interest Day. Let the children bring something from home to share that interests them.

SOCIAL STUDIES

- Study India.
- Learn about igloos.

MATH

- Learn how to measure using inches.

PHYSICAL EDUCATION

- Practice isometric exercises.

ART

- Make designs with invisible ink (lemon juice). The design will become visible when the paper is heated. Heat the paper yourself. Don't let the children do this.

J j

ATTENTION GETTER

- Put a jar full of jelly beans in the display area and ask the children if they can guess who their new animal friend is.
- Show a jump rope and ask the children who could have been jumping rope in the classroom before they came to school. Introduce Jaguar Jan.

FOOD FUN

- Make jiggling Jell-O.
- Make some jam or jelly.
- Taste different kinds of juice.

FEELY LETTERS

- Make "j's" out of jelly beans.

LANGUAGE

- Learn about jokes.
- Pattern: If I were Jaguar Jan I'd jump over _____.

MUSIC

- Listen to some jazz.
- Sing "Jim Along, Josie," "Jingle Bells," "John Jacob Jingle Heimer Schmidt."

LITERATURE

- "Jack and the Beanstalk" and "Little Jack Horner"

ART

- Make some jewelry.
- Let the children bring junk to school to make projects.

PHYSICAL EDUCATION

- Do some jumping and jogging.
- Learn to jump rope.
- Try some jumping jacks.

MATH

- Make a graph of the children's favorite jelly bean flavors.

SCIENCE

- Observe changes in Jell-O from powder to liquid to solid form.

CELEBRATION

- Throw a Jaguar Jan Junk party. Have the children bring junk to school to talk about or to make junk art with.

K k

COLLECTABLES

kale	king
kaleidoscope	kite
kangaroo	kisses (chocolate)
kerchief	kitchen
kettle	kiwi
key	koala
kimono	kumquat

ATTENTION GETTER

- A kettle can serve as a great container for things that begin with the "k" sound. Ask the children to think of an animal that begins with that sound. Introduce Katy Kangaroo.

FOOD FUN

- Make kabobs using different fruits. (Cooking will not be needed.)
- Taste kiwi fruit.

FEELY LETTERS

- Let the children make the letter "k" from popcorn kernels.

LANGUAGE

- Pattern: Kindly Katy Kangaroo likes _____ and kids too.

MUSIC

- Make and play kazoos. Form a kazoo band.
- Sing "K-K-K-Katy."

LITERATURE

- Katy No Pockets, by Emmy Payne
- Klippity Klop, by Ed Emberley
- Learn the nursery rhymes "Three Little Kittens," "Polly Put the Kettle On," and "Old King Cole."

ART

- Make kites.
- Make crayon rubbings of keys.

MATH

- Put fruit on kabob sticks in a repeating pattern.

SOCIAL STUDIES

- Learn about kings.

SCIENCE

- Learn about kangaroos and koalas.

PHYSICAL EDUCATION

- Learn to kick a ball.

CELEBRATION

- Have Katy Kangaroo's King for a Day party. Make kingly crowns and have a royal procession.

L l

COLLECTABLES

label	lemon
lace	letter
ladle	licorice
lamb	lid
lavender	lime
leaf	lipstick
leash	lollipop

ATTENTION GETTER
- Write a letter introducing Lion Lou, and put it in the library for the children to discover. Follow up each day of the study with other letters telling about the Lion Lou lessons for that day.
- Put objects that begin with the "l" sound in a lunch box in a display area. Ask the children whose lunch it might be after naming each of the objects.

SOCIAL STUDIES
- Learn about the library.

LANGUAGE
- Brainstorm about little things. Use this pattern to make up pages of a book: Ladybugs are little and so are _____
- Pattern: Lion Lou loves _____ and you too.

MUSIC
- Sing "Here We Go Loopy Loo" and "Did You Ever See a Lassie ?"

LITERATURE
- <u>Leo the Late Bloomer</u>, by Robert Kraus
- <u>The Grouchy Ladybug</u>, by Eric Carle
- <u>The Happy Lion</u>, by Louise Fatio
- <u>Dandelion</u>, by Don Freeman

ART
- Make leaf prints by painting the vein-side of a leaf and printing it on construction paper.

FOOD FUN
- Taste licorice.
- Make lemonade.

SCIENCE
- Study lions and ladybugs.
- Learn about liquids and solids.
- Compare lemons and limes.

MATH
- Balance some lemons against a described weight.

PHYSICAL EDUCATION
- Play London Bridge.
- Practice leaping many different ways.

FEELY LETTERS
- Make "l's" from long licorice ropes.
- Glue leaves on "l's."
- Glue lemon drops on "l's."

CELEBRATION
- Have Lion Lou's Leave No Litter Day. Make litter bags to use on a litter hunt around school.

M m

COLLECTABLES

macaroni	medal
magazine	menu
magnet	metal
map	milk
marble	mirror
marshmallows	mitten
mask	money
matches	

ATTENTION GETTER

- Make a frame that you call the magic mirror. Say, "I wonder whose magic mirror this is."
- Perform magic: use a magic wand and a magician's hat filled with things that begin with the sound of "m." Ask what animal might be a magician.
- Introduce Moe Monkey.

SOCIAL STUDIES

- Do a unit called "All about Me."
- Learn about mothers.

PHYSICAL EDUCATION

- Practice mime.
- Exercise to music.

LANGUAGE ACTIVITIES

- Pattern: Moe Monkey makes marvelous muddy _____.

MUSIC

- Listen to different kinds of music (rock, classical, western, etc.).
- March to famous march music.
- Sing "Here We Go 'Round the Mulberry Bush," and "The Muffin Man."

LITERATURE

- Morris's Disappearing Bag, by Rosemary Wells
- Make Way for Ducklings, by Robert McCloskey

ART

- Make mosaics.
- Make mobiles or monster masks.

MATH

- Learn about money and measurement.
- Sort, count, and graph M & M's.
- Estimate how many marbles are in a jar.

SCIENCE

- Learn about monkeys.
- Study the moon or magnets.
- Find out about magnification.

FOOD FUN

- Make muffins or macaroni and cheese.
- Taste mushrooms and melons.
- Cook meatballs.

FEELY LETTERS

- Glue macaroni on "m's."
- Make "m's" from tiny marshmallows.

CELEBRATION

- Have Moe Monkey's Merry Masquerade Party. Make masks to wear in a merry march.

N n

ATTENTION GETTER

- Introduce Narwhal Ned and his letter "n" by discussing this unusual animal. The narwhal is a member of the whale family and lives in the Arctic Ocean.

FEELY LETTERS

- Glue noodles on "n's."

LANGUAGE

- Discuss nicknames and nightmares.
- Pattern: Narwhal Ned is the nicest thing I know, and so is a _____.

LITERATURE

- Too Much Noise, by Ann McGovern
- There's a Nightmare in My Closet, by Mercer Mayer
- Never Talk to Strangers, by Irma Joyce

MUSIC

- Clap the syllable patterns in the children's names.
- Sing "I'm a Nut."

ART

- Make necklaces.
- Make nature prints.
- Decorate the letters of the children's names to create name designs.
- Make nickel rubbings.

PHYSICAL EDUCATION

- Do neck stretching exercises.

SOCIAL STUDIES

- Study nurses.
- Learn about newspapers.

FOOD FUN

- Cook and eat noodles.
- Make noodle nests from melted butterscotch chips, coconut, and chow mein noodles.

MATH

- Sort, count, and graph nuts.
- Learn to recognize numbers.
- Introduce the nickel.

SCIENCE

- Study nests.
- Learn about good nutrition.
- Find out about narwhals.

CELEBRATION

- Take a Narwhal Ned Nature Walk. Observe things in nature.

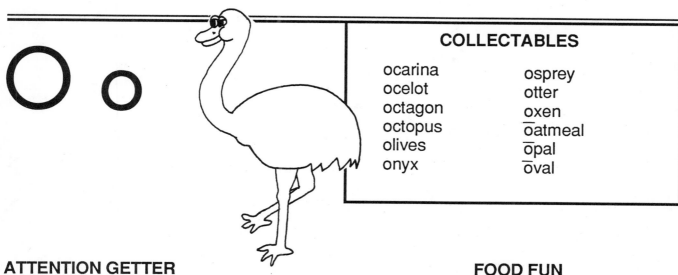

Oo

ATTENTION GETTER

- Introduce the short sound of "o" by telling about the ostrich. It is the largest living bird. The females lay eggs that weigh up to 2 1/2 pounds and can be 6 inches long.

PHYSICAL EDUCATION

- Set up an obstacle course and go through it.

FEELY LETTERS

- Glue uncooked oats on "o's."

LANGUAGE

- Brainstorm a list of opposites.
- Learn about the words "on" and "off."
- Pattern: Oliver Ostrich is odd and so is an _____.

MUSIC

- Sing "The Bear Went Over the Mountain."
- Learn about opera.

LITERATURE

- <u>Push, Pull, Empty, Full: a Book of Opposites</u>, by Tana Hoban
- <u>Over in the Meadow</u>, by Ezra Jack Keats
- <u>The Old Woman</u>, a folktale

FOOD FUN

- Make omelettes.
- Taste olives.
- Cook oatmeal or oatmeal cookies.

SCIENCE

- Study the ostrich.
- Learn about oxygen.
- Find out what is done in observatories.
- Study the osprey ocelot, ox, and otter.
- Find out about ocean life.

MATH

- Learn about the oval shape.

CELEBRATION

- Plan Oliver Ostrich's Day at the Opera. Talk about opera. Invite an opera singer to visit. Listen to parts of a children's opera.

P p

COLLECTABLES

paint	penny
paste	perfume
peach	pin
peanuts	potato
pear	pumpkin
pen	puppet
pencil	purse

ATTENTION GETTER
- Make popcorn with the children. Have them listen to the sound as it pops and imitate it with their lips.
- Put objects that begin with the sound of "p" in a purse in the display area.
- Introduce Penguin Pete.

SOCIAL STUDIES
- Study pets and their care.
- Learn about the President.
- Invite a police officer to school.

SCIENCE
- Learn about penguins.
- Study pumpkins and plant some pumpkin seeds.
- Learn about plants.

LANGUAGE
- Pattern: Penguin Pete put a __ _____ in his pocket.

MUSIC
- Listen to piano music.
- Learn about the piccolo.
- Do a polka.
- Sing "Paw Paw Patch," "Pop Goes the Weasel," and "A Peanut Sat on a Railroad Track."

LITERATURE
- Ping, by Marjorie Flack
- Pierre, by Maurice Sendak
- The Three Pigs, a folktale
- Learn "Peter, Peter, Pumpkin Eater," "Pease Porridge Hot," and "Georgie Porgie."

PHYSICAL EDUCATION
- Have a peanut hunt.

MATH
- Introduce the penny.
- Estimate the weight and circumference of a pumpkin. Then weigh it and measure it.

FOOD FUN
- Make peanut butter or pretzels.
- Cook pancakes.
- Stir up some pudding.
- Taste a fresh pineapple.

ART
- Create potato prints.
- Do penny rubbings.
- Paint pretty pink and purple pictures.
- Make pinch pots from clay.

CELEBRATION
- Have Penguin Pete's Pizza Party. Make individual pizzas.

Q q

COLLECTABLES

quart carton
quarter
quartz rock
Queen Anne's lace

question mark
quill
quilt
quince

ATTENTION GETTER
- Display a quilt or a picture of one and discuss its name, what it's used for, and how it is made.
- Introduce Quincy Quail as the animal friend who will teach the children about the letter "q."

FOOD FUN
- Taste quinces and quince jelly.
- Make quick bread.
- Taste quinine water.

MATH
- Introduce the quarter.
- Learn about the quart measure.

LANGUAGE
- Pattern: Answer Quincy Quail's question: "Do you like _____?"

MUSIC
- Listen to a quartet.

LITERATURE
- The Quarreling book, by Charlotte Zolotow

SCIENCE
- Learn about quails.
- Find out about porcupine quills.

SOCIAL STUDIES
- Study queens.

FEELY LETTERS
- Glue Quaker oats on "q's."

ART
- Make quarter rubbings.
- Make a class quilt. Each child creates a "block" from paper. Then paste the blocks on a large piece of colored butcher paper in a quilt design.

CELEBRATION
- Invite the children to Quincy Quail's quilting bee. Discuss quilts. Make a class quilt. Serve quince jelly.

R r

COLLECTABLES

rabbit	red ribbon
radio	rice
rain	rickrack
raisins	ring
rake	rocks
record	rope
rectangle	ruler

ATTENTION GETTER

- Put a small box of raisins in each child's place before school. Introduce Rhino Ruth as the animal friend who put them there.
- Get some inexpensive rings from a party supply store and put them at the children's places.

FEELY LETTERS

- Make "r's" out of ribbon.
- Cover some cut-out "r's" with raisins or rice.
- Write the "r's" with rickrack.

LANGUAGE

- Make up some riddles.
- Pattern: Rhino Ruth, Rhino Ruth, What do you read? I read about _____. That's what I read.

MUSIC

- Learn about rock music.
- Play the singing game "Ring Around the Rosie."

LITERATURE

- Read "Little Red Riding Hood" and "Rumplestiltskin."
- Recite "Rain, Rain, Go Away."

ART

- Make rubbings.
- Create rock sculptures or rock paintings.

FOOD FUN

- Make rice pudding with raisins.
- Taste rye bread.
- Cook rice and serve with butter or soy sauce.

MATH

- Use rocks for sorting, counting, and graphing.
- Learn about the rectangle.

SCIENCE AND HEALTH

- Learn about rainbows.
- Discuss rockets, rocks, roots, and rust.
- Study the rhinoceros.

PHYSICAL EDUCATION

- Hold relay races.
- Practice running.
- Learn to jump rope.
- Play Red Rover.

CELEBRATION

- Plan a Rhino Ruth Run. Designate a running course. Make runners' bibs. Run around the course for good health. Award ribbons to all the runners.

S s

COLLECTABLES

sand	spaghetti
salt	sponge
scissors	spool
seeds	spoon
skates	stamp
soap	star
socks	string
soup	

ATTENTION GETTERS
- Put a suitcase full of objects that begin with the sound of "s" in the display area.
- At Christmas, fill a Christmas stocking with "s" things.
- Introduce Suzy Seal.

MATH
- Learn about squares.
- Sort seeds.

LANGUAGE
- Brainstorm ideas about what science is.
- Pattern: Suzy Seal sees _____ in her suitcase.

MUSIC
- Listen to a soprano and a sousaphone.
- Sing "Skip to My Lou" and "Twinkle, Twinkle, Little Star."
- Listen to a serenade or a sonata.

LITERATURE
- Space Case, by James Marshall
- Swimmy, by Leo Lionni
- Stone Soup, a folktale
- Recite "Simple Simon" and "Sing a Song of Sixpence."

ART
- Create string paintings.
- Make crayon rubbings with sandpaper.
- Make paintings using squeeze bottles.

SOCIAL STUDIES
- Talk about safety.

CELEBRATION
- Hold Suzy Seal's Silly Sandwich Social. Children bring sandwich fixings. Everyone shares and creates silly sandwiches to eat.
- Suzy Seal's Super Sun Day. Children bring a variety of toppings to create ice cream sundaes.

SCIENCE
- Study snakes, seeds, skeletons, steam, space, stars, sun, spiders, or satellites.
- Learn about seals.

FOOD FUN
- Make Stone Soup.
- Taste squash and spinach.
- Create delicious sundaes.
- Make s'mores.

FEELY LETTERS
- Make "s's" by gluing salt onto an "s" shape.
- Glue sand or sunflower seeds in an "s" shape.

PHYSICAL EDUCATION
- Play Statues, Squirrel in the Tree, Steal the Bacon, and Simon Says.
- Learn to skip.

T t

COLLECTABLES

tablecloth	tissue
tack	tomato
tambourine	tongs
tape	toothpick
tea	top
teapot	triangle
tee	truck

ATTENTION GETTER

- Fill a toy truck or a treasure chest with things that begin with the sound of "t" to display. Name each one and ask the children to guess what animal's name begins the same way.
- Introduce Tiger Tim.

MATH

- Study the triangle shape.
- Learn to tell time.

LANGUAGE

- Pattern: Tiger Tim treasures _____.

MUSIC

- Listen to a tenor voice.
- Play a triangle or a tambourine.
- Learn about trumpets, trombones, and tubas.

LITERATURE

- The Enormous Turnip, by Leo Tolstoy
- Tikki Tikki Tembo, by Arlene Mosel
- Teeny Tiny, a folktale
- Recite "Tom, Tom the Piper's Son" and "Little Tommy Tucker."

FEELY LETTERS

- Make "t's" from twine or toothpicks.

ART

- Make twisted tissue pictures.

CELEBRATION

- Have Tiger Tim's Talent Time. Let the children perform for each other.

FOOD FUN

- Make tortillas, tacos, or tostados.
- Taste turnips.
- Have some tea and toast.

SCIENCE

- Study tigers.
- Learn about teeth.
- Study trees.
- Find out about tornados.

PHYSICAL EDUCATION

- Play tag.
- Walk on tiptoe.
- Practice tightrope walking with a rope that's flat on the ground.

U u

ATTENTION GETTER

- Before class, turn some things in the classroom upside down (chairs, nametags). Put other things under the tables or desks. Talk about the words "under" and "upside down." Introduce Umbrella Bird.

SCIENCE

- Learn about Uranus.

MUSIC

- Listen to ukulele music.

LANGUAGE

- Pattern: Umbrellas go up. Can_____ go up too?
- Discuss things that go up.

LITERATURE

- <u>Great Day for Up</u>, by Theo Selig
- <u>Umbrella</u>, by Taro Yashima

ART

- Make ugly pictures.
- Create U.F.O.'s to hang up.

CELEBRATION

- Umbrella Bird's Ugly Day. Let the children come to school as ugly as possible. Have an ugly face contest.

FOOD FUN

- Make an upside-down cake.

SOCIAL STUDIES

- Learn about the U.S.S.R.
- Study the U.S.A.
- Find out about UNICEF.

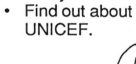

V v

COLLECTABLES	
vacuum	vinyl
valentine	violets
vanilla	violin
vase	vitamins
vegetable	volcano
velvet	vowels
vinegar	

ATTENTION GETTER

- Play some violin music. Ask what instrument is playing the music. Introduce Vulture Vic as the animal friend whose name begins with the same sound.
- Make a big valentine with pictures of objects that begin with the "v" sound on it for the display area. Tell the children that Vulture Vic sent it.

FEELY LETTERS

- Make "v's" from velvet ribbon.
  Write "v's" in vanilla pudding.

LANGUAGE

- Discuss vacations.
- Pattern: Are _____ valuable to you, Vulture Vic?

MUSIC

- Listen to the violin and the viola.

LITERATURE

- Mrs. Vinegar, by Simon Stern

MATH

- Graph the class's favorite vegetables.

SOCIAL STUDIES

- Learn about voting.
- Find out about veterinarians.
- Study Valentine's Day.

CELEBRATION

- Hold Vulture Vic's Vegetable Variety Show. Have a vegetable tasting party. Make vegetable soup.

FOOD FUN

- Taste different kinds of vegetables.
- Cook vegetable soup.
- Make vanilla pudding.
- Smell and taste vinegar.

ART

- Make vases from juice cans by decorating them with macaroni, yarn, paper, etc.

SCIENCE

- Learn about vultures.
- Study vegetables and volcanoes.

W w

COLLECTABLES

waffle	well
wagon	wheat
wallet	wheel
walnut	window
wand	witch
water	wood
watermelon	wool
web	

ATTENTION GETTER
- Put things that begin with the "w" sound in a wagon. Name each one with the children and ask them how the names are alike.
- Put a wallet in the display area with pictures in it of things that begin with "w."
- Introduce Walrus Walt.

SCIENCE
- Study weather.
- Learn about the wind.
- Find out about walruses.

FOOD FUN
- Taste watercress.
- Make whipped cream.
- Munch some watermelon.

LANGUAGE
- Hold a discussion in whispers.
- Discuss things the children wish for.
- Pattern: Where, oh where can Walrus Walt be? Looking through a window at _____ and me.

MUSIC
- Sing "Willaby Wallaby Woo."
- Listen to a waltz.

LITERATURE
- <u>Where the Wild Things Are</u>, by Maurice Sendak
- <u>The Funny Little Woman</u>, by Arlene Mosel
- <u>The Three Wishes</u>, a folktale
- Recite "Wee Willie Winkie."

PHYSICAL EDUCATION
- Have a waddle race.
- Learn to wink.

CELEBRATION
- Have Walrus Walt's Wacky Wednesday. Let the children come to school dressed in a wacky way.

MATH
- Estimate the weight and circumference of a watermelon. Check the estimates by weighing and measuring.

FEELY LETTERS
- Write "w's" in whipped cream.
- Cut "w's" from wallpaper.
- Cover "w's" with wheat berries.

ART
- Make some water paintings on the sidewalk.
- Do some weaving.
- Create some wire sculptures.
- Design wall hangings.

X x

COLLECTABLES

xylophone

ATTENTION GETTER

- Display a xylophone. Play it and talk about the beginning sound of its name. Tell the children there are no animals that start with "x" and that they are going to make one up.

LANGUAGE

- Discuss the sound of "x" at the end of words.

MUSIC

- Listen to and play a xylophone.

ART

- Have the children draw what they think Ximnerox Xan looks like.

SCIENCE

- Learn about X-rays.

CELEBRATION

- Create an "x" animal puppet from leftover puppet parts and the scrap box.

Y y

COLLECTABLES

yam
yellow yarn
yo-yo
yogurt

ATTENTION GETTER

- Hide things that begin with the sound of "y" in the school yard. When the children find and identify them, introduce Yolanda Yak as the animal friend who will help them learn about the sound of "y" at the beginning of words.

FEELY LETTERS

- Make "y's" from yellow yarn.

SCIENCE

- Study yaks.
- Learn about yeast.

LANGUAGE

- Pattern: Yolanda Yak likes _____ and you.

MUSIC

- Listen to some yodeling.
- Sing "Yankee Doodle."

LITERATURE

- <u>Yummers!</u> by James Marshall

ART

- Create yarn pictures.

MATH

- Study the time concept of a year.
- Graph the children's favorite yogurt.

PHYSICAL EDUCATION

- Practice simple yoga exercises.

FOOD FUN

- Taste some yogurt.
- Cook yams.
- Eat just the yolks of hard-boiled eggs.

CELEBRATION

- Hold Yolanda Yak's Yummy Yogurt Party. Do some yogurt tasting.

Z z

COLLECTABLES

zero
zipper
zoot suit
zucchini

ATTENTION GETTER
- Introduce Zebra Zach as the keeper in a zany zoo. Show objects or pictures of things that begin with the sound of "z."

FOOD FUN
- Taste zucchini.
- Make zucchini bread.

FEELY LETTERS
- Make some zigzag "z's" with rickrack.

SOCIAL STUDIES
- Learn about zip codes.

SCIENCE
- Study zebras.
- Learn about zoos.

LANGUAGE
- Pattern: Zebra Zach begins with "z." So does a _____.

PHYSICAL EDUCATION
- Run in zigzags.

MUSIC
- Sing "Zippedy Doo Dah."
- Listen to a zither.

LITERATURE
- If I Ran the Zoo, by Dr. Seuss.

ART
- Create a zany zoo. Let the children make the animals from clay or paper sculpture.

CELEBRATION
- Go on Zebra Zach's Zoo Trip by taking a field trip to the zoo.

PHONICS FUN

MUSICAL EXPERIENCES

Look through your music books for songs about the animals being studied. Music can add spark to the program. Let the children pretend they are the animal being studied. Make room for some of them to move like the animal that the other children are singing about.

Music is a wonderful way to gain the children's attention for a lesson. Use the Animal Rhythms' theme song to encourage the students to gather around to meet the sound puppet they are studying.

MATCH MINE

Give each child a picture of something that begins with one of the letter sounds being studied. Then hold up a picture of something that begins with one of the sounds or say the name of a letter. The children who have pictures beginning with the appropriate letter sound come forward. Each child says the sound and names the picture.

WHICH SOUND DOESN'T BELONG?

This is a good auditory-discrimination activity to fit into those moments of waiting for someone or something. It is also a great "attention-getter" at circle time. Name three words (or show three pictures), two of which begin with the same sound and one that does not. The children must decide which word or picture does not begin with the same sound as the others.

THUMBS UP

Collect pictures of things that begin with the sounds being studied, and use them to play this auditory-discrimination game. Hold up two pictures at a time. The children put their thumbs up if the objects pictured begin with the same sound. If they do not, the children put their thumbs down.

MATCH MY SOUND

To begin this game, the teacher says a word beginning with a letter sound that has been studied. The children must think of other words that begin with the same sound and say them. After a few words are offered, the teacher switches to a word that begins with another letter sound, and the children must say words that begin with the new sound. The game is a lot more fun and moves more quickly when the words are called out spontaneously without the usually required raising of the hand. This activity can be used with a class-size group or with one child at a time. It is good for review of several sounds and is an excellent way to evaluate a child's understanding of the concept of "beginning sounds."

DRAW A PICTURE

Tell the children to think of a "picture" word that begins with the sound being studied. Choose one child to whisper a word to you. Then draw a picture of the object on the chalkboard. The class guesses what the teacher has drawn, and someone is chosen to put a circle around the letter at the beginning of the name that has been written next to it.

I SPY

Show the class a letter symbol. Then call on one child to stand in front of the group and pick out something that begins with the letter symbol that was shown. The other children try to guess what the object is from clues that are given by the one in front of the class.

SOUND RIDDLES

Give the children clues about a word that starts with the beginning sound being studied. They must guess the appropriate word. For example: This is something you put on bread or toast. It begins with "j." [jam or jelly]

SECRET SHARING

Have each child bring in an object that begins with the particular letter sound being studied. Tell the children it must be kept secret in a bag and not to show the object to anyone. Then the children take turns giving clues about what is in their bags. The others have three chances per clue to guess what the article is. If the object has not been identified after three clues, it is revealed.

TWENTY QUESTIONS

This activity, though similar to Secret Sharing, is developmentally more advanced and should be used with students who are more mature than preschool or early kindergarten. Items that begin with a letter/sound being studied are presented to the class one at a time in a bag. The children ask questions which can be answered only yes or no. Only twenty questions are allowed. If the item is not identified in twenty questions, it is revealed.

BEANBAG PHONICS

A beanbag adds fun to reviewing several letter sounds. Mark some letter symbols on the floor or on a paper grid. Then let the children toss a beanbag at the letters. To win points, they must be able to say a word that begins with the letter the beanbag landed on. The children could be awarded another turn instead of a point.

SOUND DETECTIVES

This activity may be used for a review of several sounds. The teacher chooses a committee of "detectives" to search the room for objects that have names starting with one designated sound. Only the detectives know the sound. Children whose names begin with that sound may also be collected as "clues." When all of the clues are gathered, the class figures out what the common beginning sound is. Write the names of the objects on the chalkboard after the mystery letter is discovered, and invite members of the class to circle the letter at the beginning of each word.

MATCHING NAMES

This activity helps children develop auditory-discrimination skills by asking them to match the beginning letter sounds of names. Call the name of one of the children and say, "Everyone whose name begins with the same sound as [the name of the child called], please stand." The rest of the children say the standing children's names while listening to the beginning sound of each.

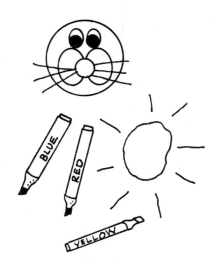

FELT MARKERS

Children enjoy writing and drawing with felt markers. As a special treat or as a project for the celebration activity, cover a table with butcher paper and provide the children with markers. Draw the puppet face and the letter somewhere on the table covering, and let the children go to work drawing things that begin with the same sound as the animal that is being studied. Use the resulting artwork as a mural, banner, or tablecloth.

QUESTION BOX

Place in a box an object that begins with one of the sounds studied. (There is a list of "collectables" on each of the activity pages.) The children ask questions about the object and try to figure out what it is. Their questions may be answered only with a yes or no.Through deductive reasoning, the children must figure out what the object is. Begin the game by telling them the sound that the object in the box begins with. When the children think they know what the object is, they ask, "Is it a _____?" If the answer is yes, the object is revealed.

FEELY PHONICS

Place various objects in a container or a prepared "feely box." Blindfold one of the children and let her/him choose an object in the container and feel it. Without seeing it or pulling it out, the child must guess the letter/sound the object begins with. Everyone must tell the blindfolded person whether or not the guess is correct when the object is taken from the box.

MANAGEMENT TECHNIQUES AND ROOM ENVIRONMENT

- <u>Animal Rhythms Area</u>

Create a space in your room just for Animal Rhythms. A "teaching bulletin board" with a small table below it is ideal. The bulletin board should have a caption representing the letter, sound, and puppet currently being studied. A large letter showing the proper formation should be displayed. The rhythm may also be included. A list of childrens' names that begin with the letter is very special. Include pictures of the real animal whenever possible. Books about the animal and real objects can be displayed on the table below. This area should be in a place where you can use it to teach from. Children can contribute to this area as well, with projects for the sound or pictures and objects shared from home.

- <u>Alphabet Charts</u>

Display your handwriting alphabet charts in conjunction with <u>Animal Rhythms</u> to provide a useful visual cue for the children. As you study each letter, put that puppet's face above the appropriate handwriting chart. By the end of your study, all of the puppet faces will be up with the handwriting charts for easy letter/sound

Aa	Bb	Cc	Dd	Ee	Ff	Gg	Hh	Ii	Jj	Kk	Ll	Mm	Nn

- <u>Rhythm Charts</u>

Make charts for each animal rhythm, so that the children can see the relationship between the words they are saying and the written symbols. The charts may also be used for the children to copy for handwriting practice when they are ready.

• Graph-a-Sound

Graphing several sounds that have been studied provides good review of beginning sounds as well as an opportunity to utilize important math concepts. Begin by rolling out a large graphing grid on the floor. (Use butcher paper ruled off in squares or oil cloth with cloth tape dividers for a more permanent graph.)

Gather real objects representing the sounds you wish to have the children practice. Place the letter and the puppet for each sound being reviewed at the top of each column on the graph. A sound object is distributed to each child. In turn the children come forward, name their object and its corresponding letter and sound, and place it in the appropriate column on the graph. Compare which puppet has more, less, or equal amounts of objects.

Mm	Ss	Bb	Gg
🧤	✂️	⚽	🍇
🔘	🥪		
🥛			
🥄			

- <u>Animal Study</u>

<u>Animal Rhythms</u> provides a natural basis from which to begin a continuous study throughout the year of animals. Collect pictures of the real animals in the program. As each sound is studied, discuss the habitat and way of life of each animal. Talk about animal families and begin to classify different types of animals.

Make a chart to represent your study of animals. Include categories representing the kind of animal (mammal, bird, reptile), where the animal lives (land, water), what the animal eats (plants, animals), how the baby is born (live, hatches from egg), and what the baby is called. As you study each letter sound, paste the <u>Animal Rhythms</u> puppet face under the categories on the chart that apply. The children will enjoy studying about the animals and have a visual tool to help them remember what they have learned.

ANIMAL RHYTHMS	Animal			Home		Food		Birth		Name of Baby
	Mammal	Reptile	Bird	Land	Water	Plants	Animals	born alive	hatches from eggs	
Mm 🐵	🐵			🐵		🐵		🐵		
Ss 🐱										
Bb 🐻										